Cornelius - a Crab with Plenty

Written and Photographed by:

Diane Baxter Trapeni

ISBN: 9798600980877

Keep an eye out for these other exciting titles:

Nellie the Nibbler

Alice the Guinea Pig

Penny the Python

Jeremiah, a Song Bird

Vincent

Hubert

Phil Harmonic

Jeff Sticks up for his Buddies

Cord, Glue and 8 Screws

A Three Piggie Circus

DEDICATION

To Ken's cousins, Bonnie and her lively family.

They know how to have fun!

DMBT

Cornelius was a pincher…

She loved to pinch your cheek, your fingers, and your wallet if she could get it!

Corny wasn't a thief, she was just mischievous!

She wasn't sneaky, she was precocious!

Adorable…not always… But she was the apple of her father's eye and she was RED!

Fast. She was fast! She could cross the sandy beach as fast as you can blink! She had to be fast or she'd be a tasty snack for a passing pigeon or a sea gull (not Scottie, of course).

Humans loved eating crabs.

She knew from all the stories her daddy told her.

Corny didn't have a mommy now and that is why.

Her mom wasn't fast enough to survive.

But that was so long ago, Corny can't remember.

What she does remember is how good her daddy is to her…every day, all day long.

Cornelius' problem is that she is so easy to spot…a flaming, red, delectable morsel on a sandy beach! Salty tasting too! No cover…No trees…No rocks to hide under…Scary! If only she had a disguise…she could dress up as a sea gull…and fly away when danger was near. Or better yet, if only she had a rocket. She'd strap it to her belly, light the fuse, and zoom around. No one could catch and eat her!

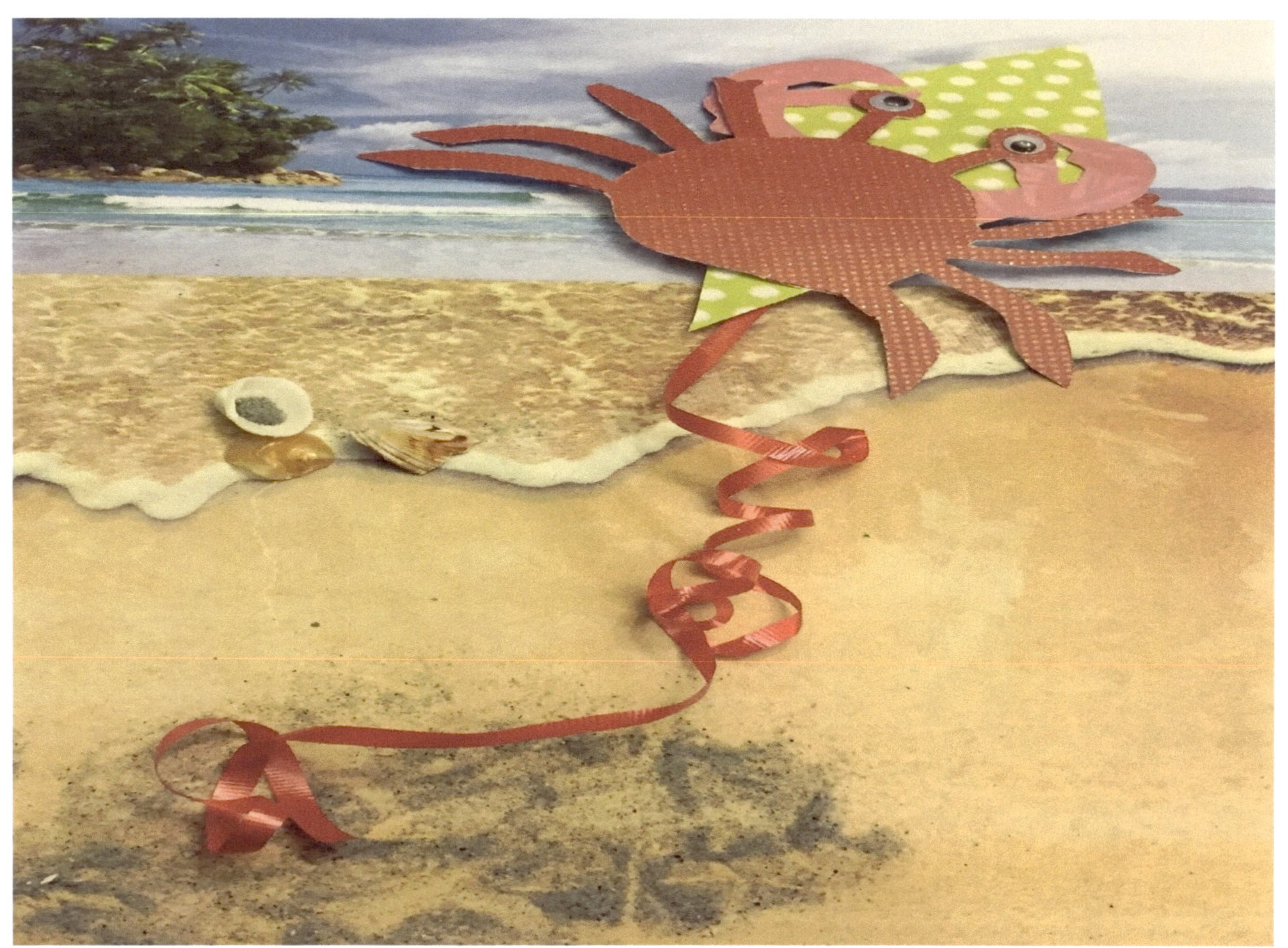

How about a kite? Lots of humans have kites
on the beach. She could tie herself to one
and go up, up, up! She could knock a few
birds out of the sky and land on a rock to hide
under. YES! She had a plan.
She figured she could get rid of all those
pesky birds by November and have the beach
to herself! Peace...Quiet...

Just then, Harold came along. Harold is a turtle. (He's on the endangered list but he's not one to tell you that!)

Harold is slow and steady…two wonderful qualities.

While Corny is fast and hurried all the time…always running for her life.

No one ever bothers Harold anymore…just Corny.

They are friends, you see.

Harold has a shell as hard as a rock to protect himself. It's a beauty.

All at once it became clear as the water before her! "Harold!" rushed Corny. "Can we hang out more?" "Like all day today, tomorrow and always?" "W-W-W-Why?" stuttered Harold. "Well, I need protection and companionship. You can protect me, hide me, travel the world with me and we'd always be together!"

Harold smiled. He felt warm all over. He, for the first time in his life, felt happy. Really happy!
He always enjoyed Cornelius' antics, sense of humor and brave way of putting herself out there in the face of danger!

Yes, they were opposites but Harold could see that Corny was not like all the rest. She had nerve and drive! "Yes!" he said proudly! "I'd be delighted to be your chaperone. Come along, Corny. Hop on and we'll enjoy our lives together!"
And they did... (Until the hurricane hit...but that's another story.)

Cornelius Ch 2

Cornelius didn't mind water…neither did Harold.
In fact, they lived in the ocean off and on. It was
the WIND! The outrageous, rushing sound of the
howling wind rising and all the debris flying by that
bothered them! There goes a door!

There goes a beach chair, towel and cooler!

Look at all those humans running for cover!

The parking lot was almost empty.

The two friends were getting alarmed.

Should they be doing something?

But what?

They had no car. They had walked.
They had no home to hide inside, or did they?
Harold offered his home to his best buddy and
together they holed up in the rocks. Seemed
safe. By nightfall, the wind died down and the
storm went from hurricane to a gentle, warm
rain. The pair had weathered a hurricane
together! They were alive and well!

By morning the beach was covered with garbage and some limping birds and other friends. There are no enemies when something horrible happens. Everyone helps out their neighbors at a time like this.

Cornelius and Harold set out to help those that were injured. Corny snipped a plastic ring off Delilah, the seagull.

Harold dragged a chair off Simone, Simon's cousin. She hardly ever goes to the beach because of the reception she gets. Everyone avoids skunks for some reason.

It took two of them to resuscitate Marge.
She was just there for a few days of sun and
fun. Maybe even a rest…but she didn't get
any yet! Marge, the hippo, thanked the duo
profusely and together the team cleaned the
beach and rescued a dozen others.

Amazing what creatures can do when they all work together on a common goal. Fast Friends for Life (FFFL) came about because of them, you know.

The End

Featuring my great nephew, Jackson Olesky, and his wonderful loving artwork. Great job! (age 8!)

We are proud to introduce:

Jules' Sleep Over

Jules loves his cousin Simon but…

Jules will not break the rules for anyone…

not even his best friend and cousin, Simon.

Would you?

Also, introducing, Kathleen Fox, the magnificent artist!

Kathleen made Jules' Sleep Over come alive!

About the TrapStone LLC: Owner and Author…

My name is Miss Diane. I taught for 42 years and have read thousands of books aloud to children.

I enjoyed that so much, I decided to write and illustrate books for you myself.

Enjoy!!!

Ken Stone Sr. is a computer programmer and a business partner extraordinaire. He put my words, pictures and computer magic together so you could meet, Cornelius, a Crab with Plenty.